I0163966

The Prepared Place

Doug Roberts

The Prepared Place
by Doug Roberts

ISBN: 978-0-9825992-7-3

Printed in the United States of America

I want to thank Laurie Thornton, Shellie Kushnerick, Rob Hatch and Fred White for all the work they did in helping me transfer the things in my heart to print.

I also want to say thank you to my wife Rita, who is the love of my life and partner on my journey.

Table of Contents

Chapter 1: Dwell

"Do not let your heart be troubled; believe in God, believe also in Me. In My Father's house are many dwelling places; if it were not so, I would have told you; for I go to prepare a place for you. If I go and prepare a place for you, I will come again and receive you to Myself, that where I am, there you may be also." —John 14:1-3

Many of us don't know that we each have a place here on Earth in which Christ has given us all authority. A place here on Earth where He has given us a portion—an allotment—to guard, rule, reign, and establish His Kingdom.

WHO IS THE FATHER'S HOUSE?

The scripture above says, "In my Father's house are many dwelling places."

Who is the Father's house? Ephesians 2:19-22 says, "So then you are no longer strangers and aliens, but you are fellow citizens with the saints, and are of God's household, having been built on the foundation of the apostles and prophets, Christ Jesus Himself being the corner stone, in whom the whole building, being fitted together, is growing into a holy temple in the Lord, in whom you also are being built together into a dwelling of God in the Spirit." So we are, as believers, part of the family of God, and we are now the dwelling place where the Father can come and live by His Spirit.

We are the house of God.

There's just one house, there's just one Kingdom, there's just one church, but there are many dwelling places. That means that God lives in each one of us individually. We are the dwelling places where God abides by His Spirit. The word "place" in the Greek is *mone*. It means "a staying, an abiding, a dwelling, abode." It's a place where God can come and stay, where God can come and live, where God can come to abide and dwell. It's us. It's you. It's me.

IN THE PLACE WHERE GOD ABIDES

"And you know the way where I am going." Thomas said to Him, "Lord, we do not know where You are going, how do we know the way?" Jesus said to him, "I am the way, and the truth, and the life; no one comes to the Father but through Me." —John 14:4-6

Now that last verse explains the gospel. There's no way to the Father except through Jesus Christ. Good works are not going to get you there. Other religions are not going to get you there. Other concepts are not going to get you there. The only way to the Father is through Jesus Christ.

Once we accept Jesus Christ as our Lord and Savior, He forgives us of our sin. Then the place He's prepared—us—is provided so that God can come down, dwell within us and live within us. Jesus has prepared us because He paid the price for our sins. He was the gift given for our sin to reconcile us to the Father. And Jesus says, "I am the way, the truth, and the life."

No one can come to the Father except through Jesus Christ.

Let's continue in verse 7: "If you had known Me, you would have known My Father also; from now on you know Him, and have seen Him."

That's so encouraging! It says, "From now on you know Him, and have seen Him." Jesus is saying that now that the Father is living within us, He is going to reveal Himself to us by His Spirit. He will no longer call us slaves—He is giving us the Holy Spirt and He will be with us forever.

Read for yourself in John 15:15—"No longer do I call you slaves [. . .] but I have called you friends, for all things that I have heard from my Father I have made known to you."

Returning to John 14, "Philip said to Him, 'Lord, show us the Father, and it is enough for us.' Jesus said to him, 'Have I been so long with you, and yet you have not come to know Me, Philip? He who has seen Me has seen the Father; how can you say, "Show us the Father"? Do you not believe that I am in the Father, and the Father is in Me? The words that I say to you I do not speak on My own initiative, but the Father abiding in Me does His works.'"

Now listen to what He's saying here. Jesus said when you've seen Him, you've seen the Father. So the words that He says to us are not words that He speaks of His own initiative, but they are the words of the Father abiding in Christ doing His works. Because of Jesus, it is the same with us! Where is the Father abiding? In us by His Spirit. Because Jesus prepared the place for the Father to come and live within us through

His death and resurrection, it is now the Father abiding in us wanting to do His works through us.

Chapter 2: Portion

Now that we understand that through Jesus Christ the Father comes to dwell within us in the power of the Holy Spirit, let's look again at the latter half of John 14:2, "I go and prepare a place." That word "place" is a different word than the previous word "place." This word is *topos*. It means, "a place, any portion or space marked off, as it were from surrounding space." It's an inhabited city, village, district. Okay, what is the place He has prepared? We know from the last chapter that He has prepared us as a place where the Father can come and live, and now that the Father is living in us, Jesus goes to prepare a place on the earth where we can walk in His authority and do the work that God has predestined us to do in Christ Jesus.

Ephesians 2:10 says, "For we are His workmanship, created in Christ Jesus for good works, which God prepared beforehand so that we would walk in them."

Now that the Father is living *in* us by His Spirit because we've accepted Jesus Christ as our Lord and Savior, Jesus has gone to prepare a place *for* us so that we can walk in the things God has predestined us to do here on the earth.

I will be with you in that place.

He says, "If I go and prepare a place." Now, remember that word "place" is *topos*, the portion, the city, the village. In other words, "If I go and prepare a [portion—a marked off space] I will come again and receive you to Myself. For where I am, there you may be also."

Get this: God is living in us because we are His dwelling place. Now that He's made His home in us, Jesus has prepared a place on earth where we can function in all that God has called us to in Christ. And Jesus says, "I will be with you in that place" because it is in Christ now that we live and move and have our being, as it says in Acts 17:28. It is no longer I but Christ in me, as we know from Galatians 2:20. The works I do are not of myself, but Christ in me working through me. Are you understanding this?

Remember what Jesus says to Philip? "The Father abiding in me does His works?" He continues in verse 11, "Believe Me that I am in the Father and the Father is in Me; otherwise believe because of the works themselves." This is another incredible verse. Jesus essentially says: If you can't believe what I'm telling you—if you can't believe what I'm saying to you—just look at the works that the Father is doing through me and in me and believe because of them.

OUR RESPONSIBILITY

Church, now that the Father is living in us and Jesus has paid the price for us, we have a responsibility to do the works of Jesus on the earth. There's a Scripture that says that as Jesus was on the earth, so we are on the earth (1 John 4:17). Whether it's in the workforce or in the ministry or in the office, whether you're a school teacher, a lawyer, a doctor, or a preacher, doesn't make any difference. The place you find yourself in is the place that Jesus has prepared for you, and you have a responsibility to do the work of God there. The Father wants to work through you to establish His Kingdom in the place where you are.

> **The Father abiding in us wants to do His work through us.**

John 14:12 says, "Truly, Truly I say to you, he who believes in Me, the works that I do, he will do also; and greater works than these he will do; because I go to the Father."

Did you understand that? Jesus said that not only are we going to do the works He did, but we will also do even greater works because He went to the Father! What's so important about Him going to the Father? He went to the Father so that the Father could have access to us! Remember? There's no way to the Father except through Jesus Christ. Jesus was obedient to what the Father required of Him on the earth, and because of His obedience and because of our acceptance of Jesus Christ, the Father can now come and live within us and do His works through us.

So now the things Jesus did we're going to do. Why? Because the Father is abiding in us and He wants to work through us to do the works He's called us to on the earth.

Chapter 3: Authority

If anyone loves Me, he will keep My words; and My Father will love him, and We will come to him and make Our abode with him. —John 14:23

I can't heal anybody. I can't save anybody. I can't do anything in my flesh that is eternal or righteous. But God in me working through me in Jesus' name can accomplish everything. People are going to be healed, saved, delivered, and set free. There's no limit to the full authority of God abiding within us!

All authority to do the work of Jesus has been given to us! As Luke 9:1-2 says, "He called the twelve together, and gave them power and authority over all the demons and to heal diseases. And He sent them out to proclaim the Kingdom of God and to perform healing." And again in Luke 10:19, "Behold, I have given you authority to tread on serpents and scorpions, and over all the power of the enemy, and nothing will injure you." Why have we been given this authority?

Because the King himself, the God of all creation, the God who holds the universe in the palm of his hand, now lives within us and wants to work through us to establish his purpose on the earth.

Because the King Himself, the God of all creation, the God who holds the universe in the palm of His hand, now lives within us and wants to work through us to establish His purpose on the earth. Isn't that exciting?

Because of Jesus' obedience, now when we respond to His love and purpose for us and we accept Him as our Lord and Savior, then the God of all creation comes and lives within us. He wants to work through us to establish what He's predestined for us. How can we fail?

Think about it: God within us is doing the work He has predestined for us. Yes! Amen!

"Whatever you ask in My name, that will I do, so that the Father may be glorified in the Son" (John 14:13).

See, we are not on the earth to glorify ourselves or build up our own ministries. Jesus isn't working to glorify us or make us whatever we think we need to be. He does what He does to bring glory to the Father in the Son. God wants to be glorified on the earth. When we allow Him to work through us to do what He wants to do, it brings glory and honor to Him, not to us.

God's a jealous God. He's not going to share His glory with anyone. God wants to be glorified on the earth and He's going to glorify Himself through His church, which is the bride of Christ, through His sons and through His daughters.

Our job and our purpose on the earth here is to fulfill the destiny that God has predestined for us in Christ Jesus.

"If you ask anything in my name, I will do it." Why? Because the Father needs to be glorified on the earth. And Jesus came not to bring glory to Himself, but to be obedient to the Father and to bring honor to the Father. Our job and our purpose on the earth here is to fulfill the destiny that God has predestined for us in Christ Jesus.

This verse says something similar: "You did not choose Me but I chose you, and appointed you that you would go and bear fruit, and that your fruit would remain, so that whatever you ask of the Father in My name He may give to you" (John 15:16).

This verse has been so misunderstood. Jesus isn't talking about whatever I need or whatever I want, but rather what is needed to accomplish what God has called me to do. I don't need a Rolex watch. I don't need a Lear jet. If I needed those things to do what God's called me to do, yes, I could ask and God would give them to me. But I don't need those things. It's not about me and what I want; it's about Christ in me. It's not about how good I look; it's about how good God looks in me working through me to accomplish His purpose.

Jesus said that everything He did, He did to bring honor to the Father. Everything He did was to be pleasing to the Father. He only spoke what He heard the Father saying. He only did what He saw the Father doing (John 5:19-20).

13

The question is: what are we doing? Are we building our kingdom or are we walking in His kingdom? Are we building our ministry or are we honoring the Father in the things He wants to do?

You have to understand that heaven and earth will pass away. The things of the earth are temporal, but the things of the kingdom of God are eternal. We're not temporal people; we're eternal people. I once heard a man say that we're not human beings encountering spiritual things, we're spiritual beings encountering fleshly things. Once we accept Jesus Christ as our Lord and Savior, we're born again. We become sons of God. God Himself comes and abides within us and we walk as new creations. We walk as new creatures on the earth. We walk as ambassadors of God on the earth, reconciling the world to Himself.

JESUS IS THE DOOR

You didn't choose Him, He chose you. He believes in you so much that He gave Jesus for you. And when you accept Jesus, then the Father can make Himself known to you, reveal Himself to you, and bring you into the fullness of who He is. Jesus, as He says, is the door.

Imagine if you invite me to your house and I knock on the door and you say, "Oh, Brother Doug, come in!"

And I say, "Oh, no, I'm just going to stand here in the doorway."

"Come on in!" you would say. "We have food. We have refreshments. Come in and fellowship."

"Oh, no, I can see inside. It looks good. It smells good. But I'm just going to stay in the door."

When we believe what He says, He who says it and is living in us will work through us to do it for us!

You would think I was strange!

But see, Jesus is the door, and a very important door at that! Jesus is an amazing door! Praise the Lord for Jesus! Without Jesus, we

15

couldn't have access to the Father. Jesus is the door into the Father. So it's time for us to come into the things the Father has for us through Jesus Christ.

RECEIVE THROUGH FAITH

God has given us faith to believe what He says! When we believe what He says, He who says it and is living in us will work through us to do it for us. Mark 16:19 reminds us, "And they went out and preached everywhere, while the Lord worked with them, and confirmed the word by the signs that followed." It can't get any better than that!

You see, faith says yes. Our faith—our yes— calls out of eternity that which Christ has already accomplished and reveals it on the earth. When Jesus hung on the cross, He cried out, *"It is finished!"* That means that everything the Father has for us to do in Christ, Christ has already done for us! It truly is finished! So through faith, we're making all that He has already done known on the earth, and we're making it known in the place He's already prepared for us! We're speaking the things He spoke, doing the things He did, and we're bringing revelation of the purpose of the kingdom of

God. When we hear the Lord and say yes, our yes confirms on the earth that which has already been done.

That's why the kingdom of God is a mystery. You can't say, "There is the kingdom," or "Here is the kingdom," because the kingdom of God is in us. It's among us (Luke 17:21). Because God Himself lives within us, the kingdom of God is every place we set our feet. Every place we go, we have authority to proclaim the kingdom of God because the King of the kingdom lives within us and all authority has been given to us who believe. Our job is to believe what Jesus did, acknowledge what the Father wants to do, and watch it happen.

Since we have now believed in Christ, let us begin to walk in that belief and take ownership of the grace, the call, and the authority of God that has been given to us in Christ.

Chapter 4: Position

I will ask the Father, and He will give you another Helper, that He may be with you forever; that is the Spirit of truth, whom the world cannot receive, because it does not see Him or know Him, but you know Him because He abides with you and will be in you. I will not leave you as orphans; I will come to you. —John 14:16-18

The Father has given us faith, He's given us Jesus, and He's given us the Holy Spirit. And with those three things, how can we fail? We've got faith to believe, we've got Jesus who has already accomplished it, and we have the Holy Spirit who is here to remind us of the things Jesus did for us and the things God has for us to do.

So many of us are walking around with an orphan mentality because we don't really know our position in Christ. We don't really know the authority that's been given to us as sons of the Father. Because we don't know who the Father is, we don't really know our identity in Christ. Part of the Holy Spirit's job is to reveal the Father to us, to remind us of our position in Christ and to make known to us the things the

Father has for us and the things Jesus has accomplished for us.

You can understand why the devil doesn't want you to be baptized in the Holy Spirit. When you're baptized in the Holy Spirit, you are brought into the spiritual arena of the Father. God is spirit and those who worship Him must worship Him in spirit and in truth.

The carnal mind and our religious traditions cannot get us into the revelation of the spirit because traditions of man are temporal and will pass away. The revelation of the Holy Spirit, however, is eternal and will last forever. As I mentioned in a

We have a different position than we had before we knew Christ: we're seated with Him in heavenly places.

previous chapter, we are eternal people in Christ. We are spiritual people. Once we accept Jesus Christ as our Lord and Savior we're no longer carnal—we're no longer flesh. We are new creations.

That's why water baptism is so important. It's a burying of the old and a rising to the new. When we are raised out of the water, we are raised up in Christ. We have a different position than we had before we knew Christ; we're now seated with Him in heavenly places. From this new place we walk in the spirit of revelation given to us by the Holy Spirit to accomplish the things that God has predestined for us.

CHRIST IN YOU, THE HOPE OF GLORY

For we are His workmanship, created in Christ Jesus for good works, which God prepared beforehand so that we would walk in them. — *Ephesians 2:10*

God has predestined us for good works in Christ Jesus. The works that God has for us are only in Christ. In Christ! The mystery of the gospel is Christ in you, the hope of glory.

We've got to come into an understanding of who we are in Christ. Once we find our place and our position in Christ, God can move and work through us to do the things He wants to accomplish in the place that Jesus has prepared for us. Remember, it's Christ in us working through us to accomplish God's purpose for us.

Ephesians 1:3-5 says, "Blessed be the God and Father of our Lord Jesus Christ, who has blessed us with every spiritual blessing in the heavenly places in Christ, just as He chose us in Him before the foundation of the world, that we would be holy and blameless before Him. In love He predestined us to adoption as sons through Jesus Christ to Himself, according to the kind intention of His will."

God predestined us to be adopted into His family through Jesus Christ. Remember? Jesus is the door to the Father. The Father wants us to come into the things that He has for us.

Let me tell you a story to illustrate this point. I have two children—I have a daughter and I have a son. When they come to my house, they don't knock on the door and say, "Hello? This is your daughter Amy," or, "This is your son Jeremy." They just come right into my house because they're my children. When they come into my house, they go to my kitchen, open up my refrigerator, eat my food, and make themselves at home. Why? Because they're my children and they know that everything I have is theirs.

If they're hungry, they say, "Mom, we're hungry. Can you fix us something?" My wife will fix them something to eat. Why? Because they're my family! They're my children!

When you go to your father and mother's home, you don't knock on the door. You go right in because their home is your home. Whatever they have is yours, and you know it.

God has given us everything and has provided for everything. It pleases Him when we respond to what He has for us by walking in it.

This is our hope as parents. Our heart for our natural children is that they'll be smarter than we were, that they'll do greater things than we did, and that they'll fulfill what God has called them to. We take pride when our children succeed and when they prosper. I think God the Father also takes joy when He sees us walking with ownership of what He's called us to do. Our confidence in our authority and position pleases Him. The Word says it pleases God to give us His kingdom (Luke 12:32). God has given us everything and has provided for everything. It pleases Him when we respond to what He has for us by walking in it.

I use an illustration when I'm out ministering: I hold up a $20 bill and I say, "It would please me to give this to you." Sometimes I have to repeat it two or three times. "It would please me to give this to you!" Eventually somebody gets up out of the congregation and takes the money out of my hand, and I say, "Hallelujah! It gave me joy to give you that!" All of a sudden it dawns on everyone else that I was serious! Unfortunately they missed out on the blessing of that $20 because they didn't believe and respond.

So many times we miss out on what God has for us because we don't think He really wants us to have it or because we don't think we really deserve it. Well, we don't deserve it! But because of Jesus Christ, it's been given to us. We can't earn it and we can't lose it. It's a free gift given to us by the Father through Jesus Christ. We just have to have faith to take ownership of it.

Chapter 5: Reveal

In that day you will know that I am in My Father, and you in Me, and I in you. —John 14:20

Once we've come into an understanding of what the Father has for us, once we come into an understanding that the Father abides within us, once we come into an understanding that all kingdom authority has been given to us, once we have a realization of who we are in Christ—that we're no longer orphans, that we're now sons and that because we're sons we've been given authority to walk in the Father's kingdom—then a whole new world opens up to us. What weapon formed against us can

Christ living within us wants to radiate through us to reveal to those around us His love, His purpose, His redemption, His salvation, and His reconciliation.

prosper? What plan of the enemy set against us can succeed? None! Why? Because if God is for us, who can be against us?

When we know the Father is living within us and wants to work through us, when we function in the grace and the gifts the Holy Spirit has given us in the place Jesus has prepared for us, then we walk in God's authority to reveal His purpose. How can we fail?

Hebrews 1:3 says, "And He is the radiance of His glory and the exact representation of His nature, and upholds all things by the word of His power."

You see, Jesus was not the reflection of the Father. Unlike the moon, which has no identity apart from the sun, Jesus and the Father are one and when you see Jesus, you see the Father. Christ living within us wants to radiate through us to reveal to those around us His love, His purpose, His redemption, His salvation, and His reconciliation.

Psalm 34:8 says, "Taste and see that the Lord is good!" There's something in us that the world is longing for! When we allow the Lord to be who He is in our lives in every place we find ourselves, the world is going to taste and see and know that God is good!

1 John 4:17 says, "As He is, so also are we in this world." Remember, He said, "When you saw Jesus you saw the Father." So when people see us, they should see Jesus. They should see the Father. They should see the nature and the character of the Father. They should see the love of Jesus. They should see the compassion and fullness of who God is because God has chosen to limit Himself on the earth through us.

Isn't that amazing? God wants to manifest Himself on the earth through you! He chose you. He called you. He appointed you. He calls you a friend.

1 John 3:1 says: "See how great a love the Father has bestowed on us, that we would be called children of God."

We are now children of God! The world doesn't recognize us or know who we are, because they don't know Him. And if they don't know Him, then they sure can't figure out who we are. If they don't know our Father, how can they know us?

But understand that we are supposed to be the reflection of our Father! When they see us they will see the Father!

Ephesians 4:29, "Let no unwholesome word proceed from your mouth, but only such a word as is good for edification according to the need of the moment, so that it will give grace to those who hear."

When they see us, they will see the Father.

2 Corinthians 5:20, "Therefore, we are ambassadors for Christ, as though God were making an appeal through us; we beg you on behalf of Christ, be reconciled to God."

Friends, how we walk, how we live, and how we talk is so important. Jesus has prepared a place for us here and now—on the earth—in order that we would function in the things the Father has for us to be and do so that He may be glorified through us and the world would be reconciled to Him.

THE EARTH IS WAITING FOR YOU!

You have to understand that these passages we're looking at in John 14 and Ephesians 2 are not talking about Jesus going to prepare places for us in heaven. We're not going to do any great works in heaven. Nobody's going to need healing in heaven. Nobody's going to need salvation in heaven. Nobody's going to need deliverance in heaven. We're going to be in the presence of the King of Kings, the Lord of Lords! We're going to be in the presence of God Himself. Who's going to need anything there? No, these scriptures are not talking about heaven; they're talking about the earth! There is a place Jesus has prepared on the earth for you to function in the things God has called you to do.

Romans 8:18-21, "For I consider that the sufferings of this present time are not worthy to be compared with the glory that is to be revealed to us. For the anxious longing of the creation waits eagerly for the revealing of the sons of God. For the creation was subjected to futility, not willingly, but because of Him who subjected it, in hope that the creation itself also will be set free from its slavery to corruption into the freedom of the glory of the children of God."

And verse 22, "For we know that the whole creation groans and suffers pains of childbirth together until now."

Do you understand what these passages say? The earth is waiting for you! The earth is waiting for me—waiting for us—to come into the ownership of who we are in Christ as sons and daughters of the Lord, to walk in kingdom authority on the earth so that the kingdom of God can be established through us in the places Jesus has prepared for each of us. I can't build the kingdom any more than I can build the church. Jesus said that He would build His church. I can't build the Father's kingdom, either! It's already established. All I can do is reveal the Father and make Him known. And the Father, through Jesus Christ, will establish His kingdom on the earth.

Chapter 6: Walk

Not that I have already obtained it or have already become perfect, but I press on so that I may lay hold of that for which also I was laid hold of by Christ Jesus. Brethren, I do not regard myself as having laid hold of it yet; but one thing I do: forgetting what lies behind and reaching forward to what lies ahead, I press on toward the goal for the prize of the upward call of God in Christ Jesus. —Philippians 3:12-14

Paul got a vision of what God had predestined him for in Christ, so he left the religious things of the world and the traditions of men in order to press in. He wanted to lay hold of what Jesus had called him to. Remember what Jesus said? *I chose you. I called you. I appointed you.*

Like Paul, I believe that when I die and stand before the Lord, I'm going to have to give an account for my life. I

True evangelism says that my Father believes in you!

won't have to give an account for all the great work I might have done, but rather how faithful I was to what He's predestined me to do—what He put me on the earth to do. If I'm going to have to give an account for it, I need to know what it is, don't I? Do you know what yours is? How faithful have you been with the gifts that He's given you in the place Jesus has prepared f you? Thankfully, it is the Holy Spirit's job to reveal your place to you and to reveal Himself in it.

Our job is simply to allow the Father who is abiding within us to work through us in Jesus' name to accomplish the works that He has predestined us to do. Recognize that wherever you find yourself—whether as a school teacher, a garbage man, a homeschool mom, or a government official—you have all authority in that place to do the works of Jesus. Remember, you're going to do the works of Jesus, and as you do those works the Father will be working through you, revealing Himself to the world. So when people see you, they will see Jesus. And when they see Jesus, they will see the Father. And then the world will know that God truly sent His son and He loves them.

This is true evangelism! Evangelism is not telling people they're going to die and go to hell. True evangelism says that my Father believes in you! He has a plan for you! Jesus paid

31

the price for you to come into relationship with my Father because my Father knows what He's planned for you and those plans are good! My Father has predestined you for a better way of life than what the world can offer you, so repent of your sins and come into a saving knowledge of the Lord Jesus Christ! Come into an ownership of the grace given to you! Come into a relationship with Him! Be baptized in the Holy Spirit so that He can reveal what God has predestined for you in Christ Jesus!

You are now the righteousness of God, created in Christ Jesus for good works, fully equipped, lacking nothing. This is who you are!

Walk with all kingdom authority in the place that Jesus has prepared for you to walk. You can be like the apostle Paul when he said, "I have run the race. I have finished my course. I have done that which God has called me to do" (2 Timothy 4:7). And then when you stand before the Lord, He can say, "Well done, my good and faithful servant" (Matthew 25:23).

My prayer is that the Holy Spirit will begin to reveal to you the place that Jesus has prepared for you, and I pray that in that place the Father will be working through you, manifesting Himself in you and around you and through you to establish His purpose that the world might know that God loves them and has a plan for them.

Group Discussion Guide

My hope and purpose for this book is to see it become seed in the rich soil of human hearts. These questions were put together to help you work these truths into your life.

1. What does it mean to be God's household?

2. Do you know the place that Jesus has prepared for you on the earth? Write it down and discuss with your close friends or community.

3. What does it mean when the Father says that it pleases Him to give us His Kingdom?

4. What are the implications of God having been the one who chose you and appointed you?
   How does this reality change your perspective?

5. What does it mean to walk as sons and not as orphans?

6. What has the Father given you to help you walk in His purpose?

7. How do we walk and act on the earth to display the love and character of the Father?

8. How do we show the love of God to the earth? What are the works of Jesus we are called to do?

www.ingramcontent.com/pod-product-compliance
Lightning Source LLC
Chambersburg PA
CBHW020444030426
42337CB00014B/1388